WEIGHT LOSS, FITNESS AND WELL-BEING FOR MEN OVER 65

Alan Avery

A complete guide for men over sixty-five on weight loss, fitness and how to gain a sense of well-being.

Blackthorn Press, Blackthorn House
Middleton Rd, Pickering YO18 8AL
United Kingdom

www.blackthornpress.com

ISBN 978 1 906259 63 1

2021

Disclaimer Notice:

Please note that the information contained in this document is for educational and entertainment purposes only. No warranties of any kind are expressed or implied. Readers acknowledge that the author is not engaging in the rendering of legal, financial, medical or professional advice.

By reading this document, the reader agrees that under no circumstances is the author responsible for any losses, direct or indirect, which are incurred as a result of the use of the information contained within this document, including, but not limited to, errors, omissions, or inaccuracies.

All rights reserved. No part of this publication may be reproduced, stored in a retrieval system or transmitted, in any form or by any means, electronic, mechanical, photocopying, recording, or otherwise without the prior permission of the Blackthorn Press.

CONTENTS

INTRODUCTION   iv

CHAPTER 1 WEIGHT LOSS

Weight	1
Diet	5
The Amount we Eat	6
The Diet Plan	13
A Day on the Diet Plan	17
Recipes	21

CHAPTER 2 EXERCISES

Exercises	24
First Week – the warm up	31
Strength Training – floor exercises	42
Strength Training – weight exercises	47
The Warm Down	56
The Jogging Programme	62
The After Jog Warm Down	71
Exercise Charts	73
Building Up to the 5 Km Jog	77

CHAPTER 3 WELL-BEING

Perspectives 79, Being Happy 82, Money 83, Sleep 84, Smoking 85, The Married Life 85, Sex 86, Retirement 87, Age 88, Death and Assisted Dying 88.

INTRODUCTION

This book is written for men over sixty-five who want to lose weight, improve their fitness and achieve a sense of well-being. Most fitness regimes are aimed at younger people who populate our fitness centres or who play a lot of sport. They have probably never suffered back-ache or had a knee give way or had stiff necks. Their time will come but for those of us in our sixties and seventies and beyond, what is needed is a fitness programme which is manageable, progressive and rewarding enough to provide the motivation we need to get up from our desks and sofas and do something positive.

This book started with a photograph. I had a mental picture of myself as a reasonably well set up average sort of man. Then I saw a photograph of myself, taken unawares by me. Who was this chubby faced, round bellied man staring out at me from the photograph? It was me. Time and a sedentary job had taken its toll on me. I was twice the man I used to be. I weighed myself and checked myself on the BMI scale (see later in the book). I was well overweight. Apart from the occasional short walk, I had taken no exercise in years. It was time to do something about it. There followed three years of research and trial and error. The result was that I lost weight and am now where I should be for my height and weight and I take regular exercise that leaves me with a sense of well-being and able to do most physical things that I want to do like swimming, jogging and playing football with my grandson.

Let me say from the start that I am not medically trained, nor do I have any qualifications in sport or athletics training. Everything written in this book comes from my own experiences in getting and staying fit and healthy to a level suitable to my age and life-style. At the time of writing, I am seventy-two and have been working on the programmes set out in these pages for around three years. There is nothing original in them. I have picked them up from books, friends and the internet.

They work for me and I hope they will work for you. Having said that, you must take medical advice if you suffer from any condition that may prevent you from taking part in the programmes set out in the following pages. Be sensible, listen to your body. If something aches or is causing you pain then stop, take a break, consult your doctor and if he gives the go-ahead for gentle exercise then restart the programme but at a lower, easier level. We are not aiming to be super athletes but to improve on what we already have.

The book concerns itself with two main topics, weight and exercise but also looks at well-being or our mental state as we get older. Again, I must emphasise that I am not trained in psychology or counselling but I am saying what works for me in the hope that it resonates with you and will work for you.

The book is aimed at men because I do not have the confidence or knowledge to say that what works for men will also work for women. Also I am based in the UK so all the examples and suggestions I make are from the UK. If you are outside the UK and think this book might work for you, then all well and good.

There are no quick fixes. I am not promising you a super fit, lean body and a dynamic personality in ten easy lessons. Quick fixes generally fall apart after a few weeks. Progress, if it is to be maintained, must be gradual and sustainable.

Of course, there will be times when because of personal circumstances, illness or even downright laziness, you will not feel like staying with the programme. Do not despair. The programmes set out in this book allow for breaks so that you can come back to them when you are feeling more motivated.

We are all living longer and working longer but there is little point in that if the extra years we are living are dogged by pain and ill-health. We should be more concerned with the quality of our senior years rather than the number of them. By making an effort with our diet and exercising we can go a long way to making our senior years more productive and enjoyable.

Getting more fit and active can be very rewarding. It not only improves our general sense of well-being but brings pleasure to ourselves and those around us as we journey through the autumn of our lives.

CHAPTER 1

WEIGHT

The general problem is, as we get older, that we put on weight. This is probably because of decreased levels of activity and eating and drinking too much. Genetics may play a part. If we had overweight parents and grandparents then there is a likelihood that we will be overweight too but this should not be used as an excuse to do nothing. The other side of the coin is that we might be losing weight. If your weight is falling noticeably, then you must seek medical advice as this can be a sign of a medical problem. I am assuming that you weigh too much and want to lose weight. The questions then are, 'how much weight do you want to lose' and 'how do you go about it?'

Being the right weight is important. If we are overweight then exercising is more difficult and the strain on our hearts and joints can be debilitating. Being overweight is also linked to heart diseases and diabetes. In 2021 64% of the UK population was overweight or obese and there was evidence that this was linked to the high rate of Covid19 cases in the UK compared to countries like Vietnam which had a much lower percentage of its population overweight.

Not only that but in an age which often judges on appearance, being overweight is seen by some as being unattractive and can be a drawback in our social lives. Being the right weight increases our chances of a healthy life and increases our self-confidence and self-esteem. There is only one way to lose weight and that is to eat a healthy balanced diet and exercise more. The type of food we eat and how much we eat is generally accepted as the most important factor in losing weight. Participating in physical activity can increase our self esteem and reduce stress and anxiety but it is only a minor factor in losing weight.

So what is the right weight for me? There are a number of guides which help to indicate what our weight should be, given our height and weight. Some require a long examination in a specialist laboratory, but we will, for the purpose of this book, go for the generally accepted one, the BMI or Body Mass Index ratio. This ratio looks at our height compared to our weight and gives us a fair indication of whether we are in the right weight range or are over or under weight. It is a suitable guide for the average man but less so for the body-builder or athlete who packs more muscle and less fat then you or me but that should be no problem for readers of this book. You need to know your height without shoes and your weight. You can use metric or Imperial measures. If you are online go to:

www.nhs.uk/live-well/healthy-weight/bmi-calculator

If you are not online go to Table 1 on the following page to work out your BMI. The weights are shown in pounds and kilograms but if you are used to thinking in Stones and Pounds then multiply your stones by 14 and add on the pounds figure. So if you are 12 st 5 lbs, multiply the 12 by 14 to give168 and then add on the 5lbs to give a total of 173 lbs.

The Chart will show you where you are in the BMI range and will help you to plot a weight in the healthy range you should be aiming at. I am 1.85m (6ft 1in) and started out weighing 95Kg (209 lbs) which put me way into the overweight category. To just get into the healthy range needed to be 83 Kg (183 lbs) which was my first target. When reached that target, I planned to lose another 3 Kg to get me more comfortably into the 'healthy weight' column and then hold that weight steady. A BMI of 25.0 or more is overweight, while the health range is 18.5 to 24.9. So with a BMI of 24.2 I just got in to the health range but then got down to 80 Kg to give a little leeway.

Another quick check is waist size. If you have a waist size of over 3 inches (94 cms) then you will need to lose some weight.

TABLE 1 Adult BMI Chart

BMI	19	20	21	22	23	24	25	26	27	28	29	30	31	32	33	34	35
Height							Weight in Pounds / Kilograms										
4'10" / 1.47m	91/41	96/44	100/45	105/48	110/50	115/52	119/54	124/56	129/59	134/61	138/63	143/65	148/67	153/69	158/72	162/73	167/76
4'11" / 1.5m	94/43	99/45	104/47	109/49	114/52	119/54	124/56	128/58	133/60	138/63	143/65	148/67	153/69	158/72	163/74	168/76	173/78
5'0" / 1.52m	97/44	102/46	107/49	112/51	118/54	123/56	128/58	133/60	138/63	143/65	148/67	153/69	158/72	163/74	168/76	174/79	179/81
5'1" / 1.55m	100/45	106/48	111/50	116/53	122/55	127/58	132/60	137/62	143/65	148/67	153/69	158/72	164/74	169/77	174/79	180/82	185/84
5'2" / 1.57m	104/47	109/49	115/52	120/54	126/57	131/59	136/62	142/64	147/67	153/69	158/72	164/74	169/77	175/79	180/82	186/84	191/87
5'3" / 1.6m	107/49	113/51	118/54	124/56	130/59	135/61	141/64	146/66	152/69	158/72	163/74	169/77	175/79	180/82	186/84	191/87	197/89
5'4" / 1.63m	110/50	116/53	122/55	128/58	134/61	140/64	145/66	151/68	157/71	163/74	169/77	174/79	180/82	186/84	192/87	197/89	204/93
5'5" / 1.65m	114/52	120/54	126/57	132/60	138/63	144/65	150/68	156/71	162/73	168/76	174/79	180/82	186/84	192/87	198/90	204/93	210/95
5'6" / 1.68m	118/54	124/56	130/59	136/62	142/64	148/67	155/70	161/73	167/76	173/78	179/81	186/84	192/87	198/90	204/93	210/95	216/98
5'7" / 1.7m	121/55	127/58	134/61	140/64	146/66	153/69	159/72	166/75	172/78	178/81	185/84	191/87	198/90	204/93	211/96	217/98	223/101
5'8" / 1.73m	125/57	131/59	138/63	144/65	151/68	158/72	164/74	171/78	177/80	184/83	190/86	197/89	203/92	210/95	216/98	223/101	230/104
5'9" / 1.75m	128/58	135/61	142/64	149/68	155/70	162/73	169/77	176/80	182/83	189/86	196/89	203/92	209/95	216/98	223/101	230/104	236/107
5'10" / 1.78m	132/60	139/63	146/66	153/69	160/73	167/76	174/79	181/82	188/85	195/88	202/92	209/95	216/98	222/101	229/104	236/107	243/110
5'11" / 1.8m	136/62	143/65	150/68	157/71	165/75	172/78	179/81	186/84	193/88	200/91	208/94	215/98	222/101	229/104	236/107	243/110	250/113
6'0" / 1.83m	140/64	147/67	154/70	162/73	169/77	177/80	184/83	191/87	199/90	206/93	213/97	221/100	228/103	235/107	242/110	250/113	258/117
6'1" / 1.85m	144/65	151/68	159/72	166/75	174/79	182/83	189/86	197/89	204/93	212/96	219/99	227/103	235/107	242/110	250/113	257/117	265/120
6'2" / 1.88m	148/67	155/70	163/74	171/78	179/81	186/84	194/88	202/92	210/95	218/99	225/102	233/106	241/109	249/113	256/116	264/120	272/123
6'3" / 1.91m	152/69	160/73	168/76	176/80	184/83	192/87	200/91	208/94	216/98	224/102	232/105	240/109	248/112	256/116	264/120	272/123	279/127
6'4" / 1.93m	156/71	164/74	172/78	180/82	189/86	197/89	205/93	213/97	221/100	230/104	238/108	246/112	254/115	263/119	271/123	279/127	287/130
		Healthy Weight						Overweight						Obese			

A note about weighing yourself. Make sure you do it at the same time of day so that you are comparing like with like. First thing in the morning after going to the toilet is a good time. Do it naked so that different clothes weights do not interfere. You weigh less in the morning before the daily meals kick in so it is also a good morale boost.

So if you come into the overweight or obese category, you need to set yourself two targets. First, a maximum weight that gets you into the normal range and then a weight below that to get you comfortably into the normal range. If you are already there well done but the advice on diet still applies.

Please note that the diet and exercise programme run together. You should be doing the exercise programme at the same time as the diet programme if you need to lose weight. One will support the other. As you lose weight, exercise will become easier and as you exercise more, weight loss will be more manageable.

To repeat then, we must set ourselves two weight targets if we are overweight or obese.

1. The maximum weight I can be to get in to the normal BMI range. Write it in this box here:

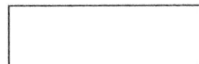

2. My ideal weight which gets me comfortably in to the normal BMI range. Write it in this box here:

There is no specific time scale for reaching these targets, although you might want to have one in mind. It might take up to two years to get in to the top end of the normal range and then up to another year to get further into the normal range. It all depends on your own circumstances. If you are in the obese BMI range then you are likely to need more time. If you are not far off then a shorter time scale is appropriate. Birthdays are good goals to aim for. 'I want to be 83 Kg when I reach 70' was my target (I just made it).There will be times when weight goes up because of holidays, birthdays or even the weekend, when there are more temptations. Don't let a weight gain on these occasions put you off. As long as you think in the long term and keep to the suggestions set our below, these blips in your weight will even themselves out.

Diet

Having a healthy diet is the main factor in losing weight and fighting off the ailments that come with obesity. Eating healthily increases our energy levels, helps us look younger, improves our immune system and helps fight low-grade inflammation.

If we are overweight or obese the likely reasons are that we are eating too much and eating the wrong kinds of food. We need to eat smaller quantities and eat food that not only satisfies our hunger but is good for us and is not full of calories that make us put on weight.

I am not going to recommend some magic diet like eating only one kind of food or substituting real food for a diet drink or biscuit. That sort of regime might work in the short term, simply by reducing your calorie intake but this is not sustainable and you will probably regain any weight your might have lost in the first place. After all, you have had several decades to find the type of foods you like to eat and decades of bad habits are not reformed in a few weeks. Plan for the long term. Make gradual but manageable changes that do not put a strain upon your body or your will-power. If you have a partner or children, then you have more than likely built up eating habits that everyone in the household enjoys. You may well have compromised what you like for the general good. That is not going to change overnight. Coming in to the kitchen and announcing that you are going on a special diet will put a strain on everyone. The best thing is if your partner, if you have one, can agree to help you and perhaps even go on the same diet as you.

The amount we eat

The first thing we can do is look honestly at the actual amount we eat. When we eat, our body uses some of the calories we consume for energy. The rest is stored as fat. Consuming more calories than we can burn may cause you to become overweight. After all, if we are overweight or obese this means we are eating more than our body needs for normal functioning. Looking honestly at the amount we eat, the pile of food we put on our plate, should mean weight loss without having to make drastic changes in our diet. Make small changes to begin with. Take five potatoes instead of six. Take a slightly smaller portion of chips than you usually do. Just have one piece of apple pie for pudding rather than two. Small changes like these will help us towards those weight targets we set out earlier.

Research has shown that using smaller plates or glasses cuts down on the amounts we eat and drink so if you use large dinner plates or large wine glasses for example, use smaller ones and see if that has any effect.

Sugar is a real enemy. If you take it in your tea or coffee or sprinkle it on your breakfast cereal then you need to try and cut it out. Again, don't simply stop taking it from one day to the next, unless you have iron will-power, or you will start craving it. If you take two spoonfuls of sugar in your tea, make the second one a level teaspoon rather than a heaped one. Gradually cut down that second tea spoon until you are down to one and then start reducing that one. Take your time. Spread the reduction over weeks or even months rather than days. That way the change will be long-lasting.

One of the problems with sugar is that it is in much of the food we eat without us even realising it. Bought biscuits and cakes, sweets and chocolate are full of it if you read the ingredients on the packet. One way round this is to start making your own cakes and biscuits and that way you can cut down the amount of sugar in them. Just start by putting in slightly less sugar than the recipe recommends. You won't notice the difference and then continue to reduce the amounts you use next time you bake. If baking isn't your thing then look at the ingredients on the packets you buy. Go for the ones with lower sugar content. Look at the traffic light system on the packet and go for the ones with green lights for both sugar, salt, fat and saturates.

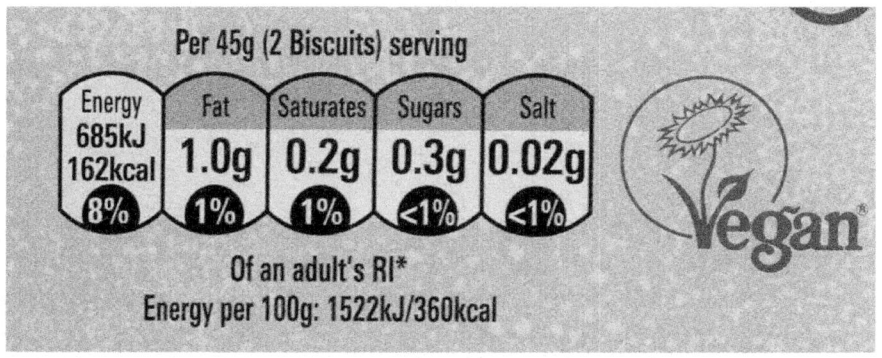

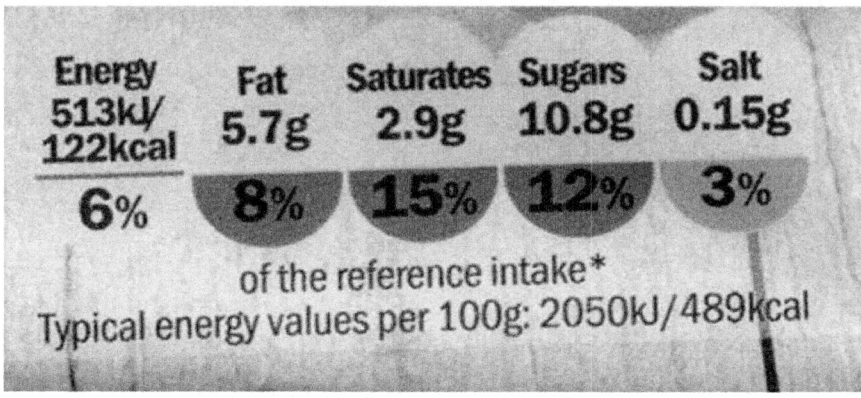

The difference in the traffic lights for a packet of Shredded Wheat (top) and a packet of biscuits (below)

It is best to avoid fizzy drinks. They contain sugar and even the ones which claim to be 'sugar free' or 'sugar reduced' are best avoided.

Some breakfast cereals have too much sugar and chocolate to tempt children. Go for Weetabix, Shredded Wheat, porridge, Bran Flakes, Fruit and Fibre and Muesli made without added sugar. In fact, any cereal that doesn't contain sugar.

You can also help by using low fat milk on your cereal and in your tea and coffee. There are now many non dairy drinks made from oats, almonds, or soya which you might like to try. Best of all is if you can drink tea or coffee without any milk.

These are some of the general things you can do to lose weight gradually. Eat smaller portions and reduce sugar and animal fats from your diet.

Let's look now at some specific suggestions for losing weight by adapting the type of food we eat. Again, I am not suggesting we go for whole-sale changes immediately. A sudden change of diet will set up cravings in the body for the things we are missing. Start by changing just one breakfast a week combined with changing one lunch on a different day. Keep this going until your are comfortable with it. Then add another changed breakfast or lunch and so on. Aim to have the recommended breakfast and lunch Monday to Friday in a reasonable time frame, say six months but, as ever, depending on your own circumstances. If you need more time, take it.

Table 2 on page 10 will help you keep check of this plan. Mark in now the day you intend to change one breakfast and the day you intend to change one lunch. Leave at least two days in between them. Stick with this until you feel comfortable with the change. Then mark in another breakfast or lunch and stick with this until you feel comfortable again. Keep on adding breakfasts and lunches until the table is full. Weekends are optional so eat what you would normally eat but you should find that the eating habits formed during the week will influence what you feel like eating at the weekend. It could take weeks or even months to fill in the table but there is no rush. Go at a pace that is suitable for you and does not cause you any discomfort or cravings.

You will see that there are two copies of Table 2. The second one is to cut out and put in a prominent place in your kitchen such as your fridge door. It will act as a constant reminder of where you are at and where you are aiming to be. It will also keep others in touch with your programme so that they can support you. There are boxes to fill in your two weight targets, just as a reminder.

Table 2

Meal Chart

	Mon	Tue	Wed	Thur	Fri	Sat	Sun
Breakfast							
Lunch							

WEIGHT TARGET 1 [ ] WEIGHT TARGET 2 [ ]

------ ✂ ------

Table 2

Meal Chart

	Mon	Tue	Wed	Thur	Fri	Sat	Sun
Breakfast							
Lunch							

WEIGHT TARGET 1 [ ] WEIGHT TARGET 2 [ ]

The Diet Plan

Here then is a diet plan which will lose you weight if you follow it. Water is given as an optional drink but it is recommended that you drink water throughout the day to keep hydrated.

Breakfast

A small bowl of one of the recommended cereals (see above) with semi-skimmed or low-fat milk or one of the non dairy options.
One piece of toast made with whole grain bread. Spread with an olive oil spread and honey or a thin layer of marmalade or jam.
OR a larger bowl of cereal without the toast.
Tea or coffee with semi-skimmed or low fat milk if needed.

Weekend Breakfasts

Treat yourself to a cooked breakfast at the weekend if you fancy it. Grill your bacon and fry your eggs in olive oil.

Mid morning

With your mid morning tea or coffee, have one or two pieces of fruit and a half litre glass of water. You should aim to eat at least two pieces of fresh fruit a day.

Lunch

Lunch can be made up of any one of the following eaten with whole meal bread, rye bread or crisp bread with a thin layer of olive oil spread. Try and cut out white bread if this is what you normally eat. Limit yourself to one piece of bread or roll.

Baked beans on toast. Watch out for some of the tinned baked beans as some of them have added salt and sugar.

Wholemeal toast with ham, spinach and a poached or scrambled egg.

Bulgur wheat salad (see recipe 1) with chicken or turkey or lean ham and a slice of whole grain bread.

Beetroot salad (see recipe 2) with a hard-boiled egg, a slice of ham and a slice of whole grain bread.

A green salad consisting of lettuce, cucumber, seed sprouts, celery pieces of pepper, cheese and a slice of granary bread.

Granary bread toast with sardines or pilchards or mackerel eaten with a green salad or beetroot salad.

Homemade vegetable soup (see recipe 3) eaten with a multi-grain roll followed by cheese and biscuits. Tinned soup can be used for convenience but again, mind some of them as they have added salt or sugar.

Drink plenty of water with your lunch.

Mix and match any of the above so that you don't leave the table hungry.

Mid afternoon snack

If you start to feel peckish mid afternoon then with your tea or coffee or glass of water, have a digestive biscuit or similar or better still some mixed nuts (not peanuts) or a piece of fruit. Dried figs, apricots, raisins and dates make a nice change.

Dinner

I make no specific recommendations about the evening meal. With a growing number of people eating vegetarian or vegan diets there needs to be a good deal of flexibility. Eat what you are used to but remember the caution about portion sizes. Your meal should include two or more types of fresh vegetables but what you have with them is down to you. Grill your meat rather than fry it.

If you regularly have take-away meals try and limit these to one a week and that includes fish and chips.

Puddings are nice but try and avoid anything with too much sugar. Cheese, yoghurt, fruit and milky puddings are a good alternative.

Alcohol

Drinking too much alcohol can slow down your weight loss. Alcohol can cause weight gain in four ways: it stops your body from burning fat, it is high in calories, it can make you feel hungry and can lead to poor food choices.

A small glass of wine contains 85 calories, a single measure of spirits 52 calories and a pint of beer 220 calories.

The UK Department of Health has set out some useful guidelines. Whilst stressing that there is no apparent 'safe level' it recommends drinking no more that 14 units of alcohol a week and that these should be spread out over three or four days.

In real terms, a pint of lager is 2 to 3 units, a pint of beer 2.2 units, a pint of cider 2.6 units, a shot of spirits 1 unit, a glass of red wine 1.8 units and a glass of white wine 1.4 units.

If your present consumption is more that 14 units a week, the best advice is to reduce your intake slowly. Try and have at least two alcohol free days or limit your drinking to the weekend.

A typical day on the diet plan

So on the following pages is a typical week-day's diet. To build up to eating like this every day can take time. Don't rush it. Introduce changes to your diet slowly.

A Typical Day on the Diet Plan

Breakfast

A small bowl of fruit and fibre cereal with oat milk.
A slice of whole meal toast with jam.
A cup of tea or coffee with semi-skimmed or oat milk.

Mid morning

One or two pieces of fruit.
A large glass of water.
Cup of coffee or tea.

Lunch

A bowl of home-made vegetable soup sprinkled with paprika. (See recipe 3)
A whole-meal roll lightly spread with olive spread.
A glass of water.

Mid-Afternoon

A cup of tea
A dozen mixed nuts and two dried figs and a date.

Dinner

A turkey schnitzel
Roast potatoes
Broccoli, carrots and green beans lightly boiled
A bowl of natural yoghurt with blueberries and a sprinkle of muesli
A glass of water or a small glass of wine or beer at the weekends.

Late Evening

A cup of non-caffeine tea without milk and a digestive biscuit.

Ideally, it is best not to eat anything after your evening meal but if you need something have a slice of toast or a digestive biscuit or a piece of dark chocolate. For a drink, mint tea, red bush or other non-caffeine drink is recommended.

RECIPES

1. Bulgur wheat salad

Ingredients

160 grams of Bulgur Wheat
150 ml boiling water
2-3 spring onions, finely chopped
2 ripe tomatoes, skinned and chopped
40 grams dried apricots, chopped
½ lime, grated rind and juice
30 ml olive oil
½ tsp honey
2 tbsp fresh coriander, chopped
1 tbsp fresh mint, chopped (optional)
20 grams sunflower seeds
40 grams black pitted olives, sliced
Pinch of salt

1. Put the bulgur wheat into a bowl and add the boiling water and then leave to cool
2. Combine the bulgur wheat with other ingredients, adding the coriander and mint last
3. Cover and leave in the fridge for at least 1 hour before eating

2. Raw carrot, Beetroot and pomegranate salad

Ingredients

Equal weights of fresh beetroot and carrot, e.g. 300 grams of each, shredded
The juice of ½ lemon
The juice and seeds of a whole pomegranate
Mix together, cover and leave in fridge before eating

3. Vegetable Soup

Ingredients

You can use any mix of vegetables to make soup.
For example
1 medium onion, chopped
1 clove of garlic, finely chopped
1 leek, sliced
1 medium potato, chopped
2 sticks of celery, sliced
1 carrot, chopped

Heat 2 tbsp olive oil in a saucepan
Add all the vegetables and sauté until soft, 5-6 minutes
Add 500 ml stock and a handful of red lentils
Cover and cook for 30 minutes
Allow to cool, then liquidise
Add salt and pepper to taste
Any vegetable can be used, sweet potato, parsnip, celeriac, butternut squash or red/yellow pepper

CHAPTER 2

EXERCISE

Taking the right exercise and the right amount of exercise is important. It should boost your energy levels, help you sleep better, improve your posture, charge up your sex drive and help combat mood swings and anxiety.

The following programme of exercises is progressive. They start at a point which assumes no previous regular exercise has been taken and ends with a series of exercises designed to keep you in condition and able to jog 5 km. You might well not reach the end of the programme. This is not unusual. Get to a point in the programme where you are not straining or in any discomfort but where there is enough of a challenge to get your heart beat raised or you are breathing harder than normal.

On the other hand, you might feel at the end of the programme that you want to go further. That is fine and suggestions are made as to how you can continue.

As has been advised previously in this book, the exercises should run in tandem with your weight loss programme so that each supports and enhances the other.

If you find that the opening exercises are too easy for you and represent no challenge, then move on through the programme until you reach a point which does challenge you and then work from this point forwards. Don't move on to the next phase until you are comfortable with the stage you are at. This is not a competition or a race. The exercises are designed to tone your muscles not to make you a body-builder or weight-lifter. Don't jump over any part as you will miss the instructions to each exercise.

We are working on a two week cycle which consists of three days when there will be floor and weight exercises you can do at home and two days when you will be walking and later jogging. There is no set pattern for these exercises but you must leave at least one day, preferably two days between the walking and jogging exercises and the floor and weight exercises. Ideally you should fit everything in Monday to Friday leaving the weekends free to relax. However, if you are working, you might find it more convenient to include one or two of the weekend days.

The programme will look something like the charts over page. There is a blank programme for you to write in what is best for you. If, for whatever reason, you miss a day, just pick up on the next convenient day. If you miss more than one day and are finding it hard to pick up where you left off, then go back down the programme to a point where you can comfortably manage again.

Any exercise programme consists of three parts: the **warm up** then the main **strength training** combined with alternate **endurance training** and finally the **warm down**.

The Warm Up

This consists of a series of exercises which are designed to stretch and 'warm up' all the main muscle groups so that when we come to do the strength training and endurance training they are easier to manage and we are less likely to pull or strain a muscle. They are important so never skip them.

Table 3	Exercise Programme		First Week			
Monday	Tuesday	Wednesday	Thursday	Friday	Saturday	Sunday
Floor Exercises	Walk / Jog	Weights Exercises	Floor Exercises	Walk/Jog	Rest	Rest
			Second Week			
Weights Exercises	Walk / Jog	Floor Exercises	Weights Exercises	Walk / Jog	Rest	Rest

Table 3	Exercise Programme		First Week			
Monday	Tuesday	Wednesday	Thursday	Friday	Saturday	Sunday
						t
			Second Week			

Strength Training

We build up our strength using a series of exercises which make demands on our muscles. By repeating exercises and building up the number of times we repeat them, we gradually build up our body strength. Using weights are an important part of this strength training and you will see from Table 3 that we alternate between floor exercises such as press ups and weight training using weights.

Endurance Training

This can be walking, jogging, swimming and biking or playing tennis. These are all exercises which will improve your circulation and lung capacity and build up the amount of time you can carry out these activities. Swimming is particularly beneficial if you suffer from joint pains as the warm water and buoyancy of the water takes pressure off the joints. This book uses walking and jogging as the endurance part of the programme but if you enjoy swimming and biking then do them as an alternative to walking and jogging, perhaps at the weekend when you have some free time.

The Warm Down

As its name suggests, the warm down is a series of exercise done after strength training and endurance training to make sure our muscles are fully relaxed. They help prevent cramps and stiff muscles.

Time

You will need around half an hour a day for the floor and weight exercises and a maximum of two hours for the walk or jog but this won't be until the end of the programme. The initial walks and jogs are shorter than this. So think about your daily routine. When can I conveniently fit these times in? Best not to do them just after a meal.

Try and build up a routine when you do the exercises at around the same time each day. I jog early afternoon and do the floor and weight exercises around 5 pm before dinner but everyone is different and you will need to plan what is best for you.

Tread mills or the great outdoors?

There are advantages to using a tread mill rather than going outside and taking your exercise. They are weather proof. It takes a certain amount of determination to set off for your jog when it is cold or raining but after a while, if you are wearing the right clothes, this can actually be enjoyable.

On the other hand, buying a good quality machine or joining a gym can be expensive and actually being outdoors rather than in your bedroom is therapeutic. I tend to jog around the same two or three courses, sometimes clockwise sometimes anti-clockwise and seeing the fields change as the new crops come through, the flowers bursting through in the spring and the trees coming into leaf in the summer and the autumn colours is a delight and a wonder. Also, I am in control of the jog. If I want to slow down a bit I can. If I am feeling good on a particular day, I can lift my tempo. Of course, you can do this on a machine by twiddling the knobs but it's not the same. It's up to you but you can see what I prefer.

If you do opt for a machine then go for one that does not have an electric motor but one that lets you set the pace naturally. It should, however, have a distance counter so that you can monitor the distances you are going.

I am lucky, living in a small town. I can set off from my front door and in ten minutes I am out in the open countryside. If you live in a city, then explore your local park as a place to exercise or if it does come down to a choice between a jogging machine in your bedroom with the window open or risking the traffic and pollution of a large city, then stay indoors with the machine. A compromise would be to have a machine and use it when the weather is bad or time is short but to go outdoors when the weather or time allows.

A point to note if you exercise outdoors is stay on the pavement or tarmac road. Rough ground is an ideal place to twist your ankle or worse still, fall over and do some real damage. If you can, let someone know where you are going and when you are likely to be back. Take a mobile phone with you if you have one, just in case.

What should I wear?

If you are indoors in your own home wear what you like. A T shirt and underpants and barefoot works fine. Once you are outdoors in public then you need to wear something suitable. The most important item is footwear. For walking a strong pair of ordinary shoes or trainers is fine but when we progress to jogging it is essential to get a decent pair of running shoes. They will support your feet and be light enough to enhance your performance. Make sure they fit well. Go to a shop and try them on if you can but if buying on line, make sure it is from a firm that allows returns so that you can send back anything that turns out to be too small or too large.

You will also need a running vest, shorts, running socks and a woollen hat for the cold weather or a cap for when the sun shines. Get proper running clothes not just your usual cotton T shirts; these hold the sweat and the rain and do not dry out properly. The picture above shows the type of clothes you should be wearing. If you are using a running machine at home, then wear what you like, of course, but I would still advise against cotton clothes.

FIRST WEEK

The Warm Up

We are going to start off with twelve 'warm up' exercises. They will give the body a good stretch and get us ready for the strength training to follow.

(a) (b) (c) (d)

Exercise 1. Body Stretch

(a) Stand up straight with your hands cupped in front of you, feet shoulder width apart. (b) With your body fully relaxed, bend over and see how close to the ground you can get your cupped hands. As you bend down, take a deep breath. Legs kept straight, not bending. Don't worry if you can only reach a short way down. You will get closer to the ground as we progress. (c) After a second or two, slowly raise your arms, turning your hands over and back behind your head, exhaling as you go up. Stretch your whole body. Clench your buttocks and feel the stretch in those nice straight legs. (d) Back to the start position. That's one movement. Let's see if you can do this five times. If you manage less than this, don't worry but see how many you can comfortably do. The final target to aim for is twelve stretches. Keep a record of how many stretches you do on the following table. If you manage all twelve, then concentrate on the quality of your stretches. Reach further down towards the ground and stretch further back. Take it easy. Don't strain anything.

1	2	3	4	5	6	7	8	9	10	11	12

Exercise 2. Neck Muscles 1

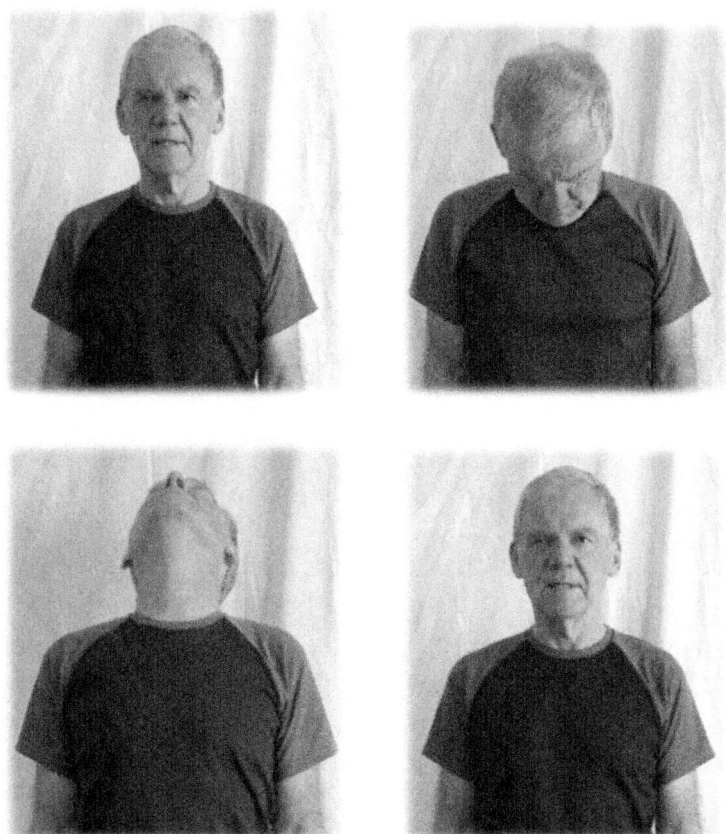

This exercise is for the neck muscles. Feet shoulder width apart, hands by your side. Push your chin on to your chest and then lift it off and stretch your head back as far as it will go. Then back to you chest and repeat this movement up to twelve times. If you don't manage the full twelve, keep a record of what you manage below and try and improve on this the next time. Try curling your tongue against the roof or your mouth as you stretch back.

| 1 | 2 | 3 | 4 | 5 | 6 | 7 | 8 | 9 | 10 | 11 | 12 |

Exercise 3. Neck Muscles 2

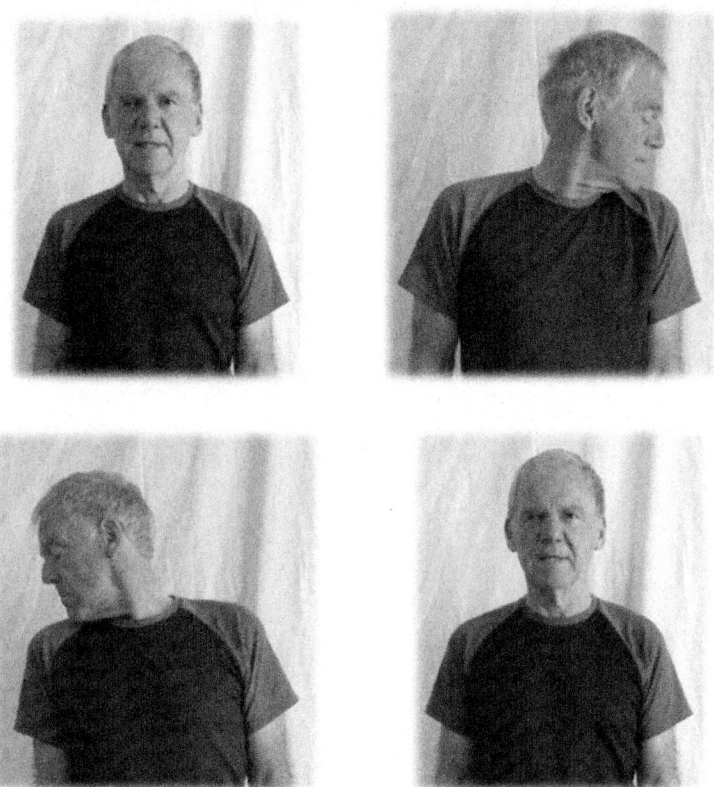

Again for the neck muscles, turn your chin to the left and try and touch your left shoulder. Then to the right and so on. Aim for twelve times in all.

| 1 | 2 | 3 | 4 | 5 | 6 | 7 | 8 | 9 | 10 | 11 | 12 |

Exercise 4. Neck Muscles 3 Head rolls

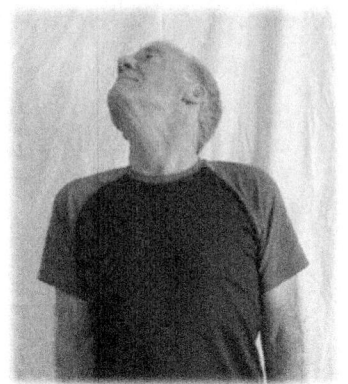

Roll your head six times to the left and then six times to the right. Aim for twelve in all.

| 1 | 2 | 3 | 4 | 5 | 6 | 7 | 8 | 9 | 10 | 11 | 12 |

Exercise 5. Arm swings

Stand with your left foot forward, all your weight on your left foot. Swing alternate arms. For the first six swings, your arms should be parallel to the floor but make the last six swings as high as you can. Aim for twelve in all.

| 1 | 2 | 3 | 4 | 5 | 6 | 7 | 8 | 9 | 10 | 11 | 12 |

Exercise 6. Side stretch

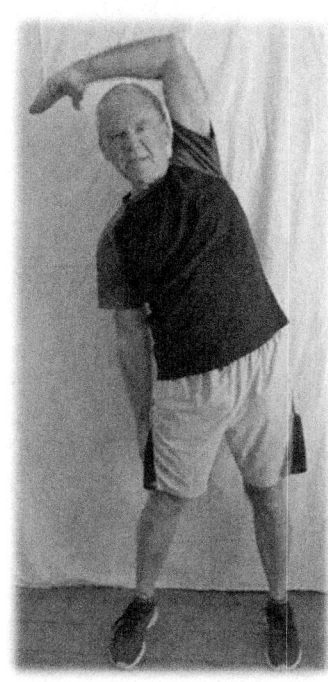

Feet shoulder width apart. Stretch your right arm over your head as far as you can while your left arm goes as far down your left leg as far as it can. Hold for the count of twelve or as long as you can. Repeat with your left arm going over and your right arm stretching down for the count of twelve.

| 1 | 2 | 3 | 4 | 5 | 6 | 7 | 8 | 9 | 10 | 11 | 12 |

Exercise 7. Dips

Feet shoulder width apart, hands on hips. Bend the whole of the upper body forward from the waist, trying to get it parallel to the ground. Take this one easy; go as far over as you comfortably can but the final aim is to be parallel to the floor. Hold for a second and then return back up. This time dip to the left, hold for a second and return back up then dip to the right, dip to the centre and so on. Aim for twelve in all.

1	2	3	4	5	6	7	8	9	10	11	12

Exercise 8. Leg Stretch 1

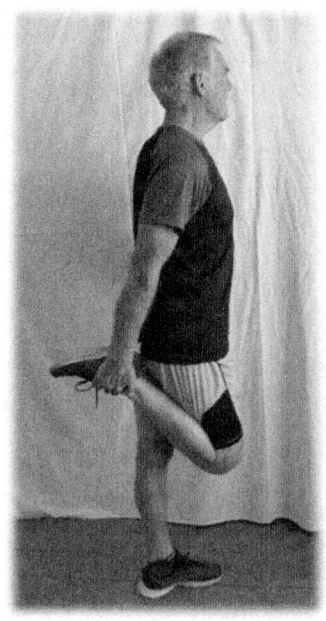

Stand feet together and then raise your right leg behind you taking hold of your foot with your right hand and bringing the heel of your foot as close to the right buttock as you comfortably can. Hold for the count of twelve or as long as you can. Repeat with the left leg. Use a chair or wall to keep your balance if needed.

1	2	3	4	5	6	7	8	9	10	11	12

Exercise 9. Leg stretch 2

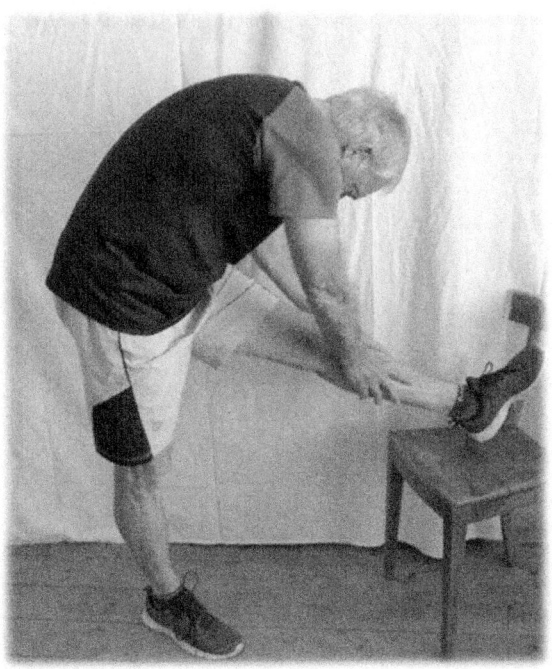

Stand in front of a chair and put the heel of your left foot on the chair, keeping your right leg straight. Now stretch your hands down the side of your leg as far as you comfortably can, bringing your head down on to your leg. Hold for the count of twelve or as long as you can. Repeat with your right leg.

1	2	3	4	5	6	7	8	9	10	11	12

Exercise 10. Leg stretch 3

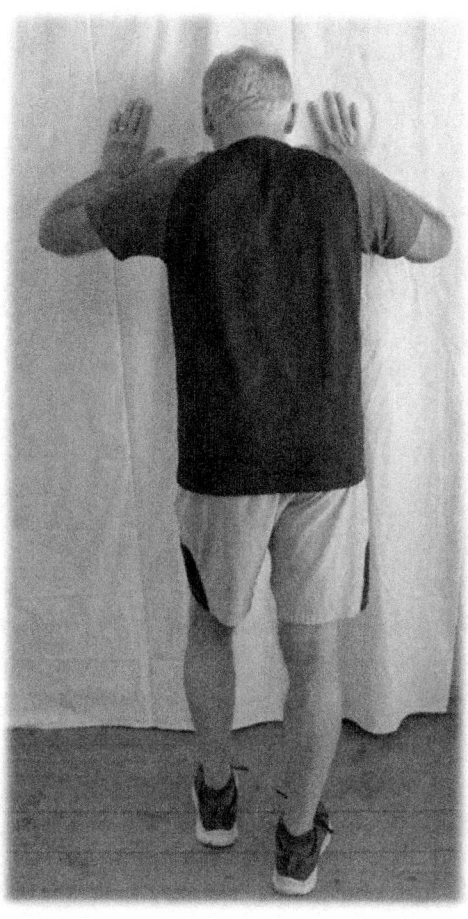

Press both hands against a wall or door frame at chest height and then step back with your right leg. Push down on your right leg and push against the wall. Hold for the count of twelve or as long as you can. Repeat with your left leg.

1	2	3	4	5	6	7	8	9	10	11	12

Exercise 11. Side stretch

 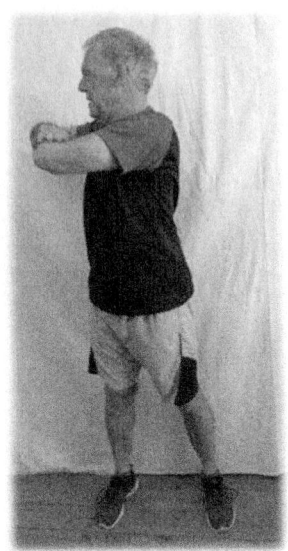

Stand feet shoulder width apart with arms folded at chest height. Twist as far as you can to the right for the count of twelve or as long as you can, back to the centre and then to the left for the count of twelve or as long as you can.

1	2	3	4	5	6	7	8	9	10	11	12

Exercise 12. Body press

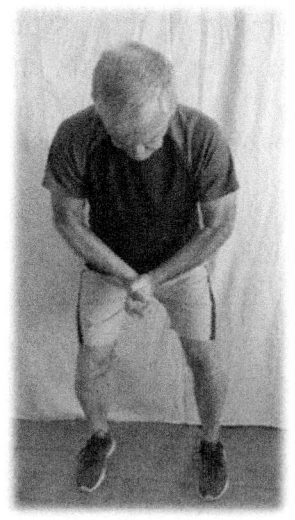 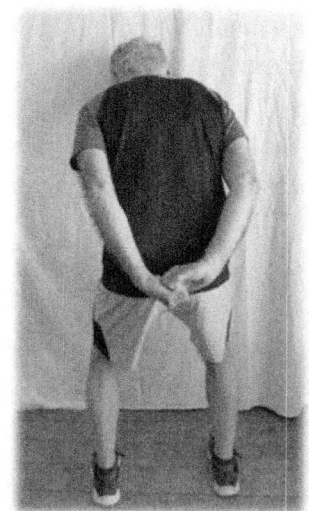

Stand feet shoulder width apart in a crouching position and hands clenched at waist height. Push your hands together as hard as you can for the count of twelve or as long as you can, tensing your whole body. Repeat with hands behind your back but trying to pull the hands apart rather than pushing, for the count of twelve or as long as you can.

1	2	3	4	5	6	7	8	9	10	11	12

STRENGTH TRAINING FLOOR EXERCISES

Now we are nicely warmed up it is time to go straight on to the strength training. You will see from the exercise programme chart on page 22 that we alternate two types of strength training. We alternate between floor exercises and weight exercises. *Don't be tempted to do both on the same day.*

Floor Exercise 13. The press up

We are aiming to do as many full press ups as we can given our strength and age. I got to 36 press ups in my sixties but am down now to 24 in my seventies and this is fine.

If doing a full press up is not possible straight away, then build up to it by aiming to do twenty wall presses, (exercise 13a) then twenty kneeling presses (exercise 13b) and then going on to full press ups.

Floor Exercise 13a. The wall press up

Stand feet together away from a wall with your palms flat on the wall. You should be at an angle of 45° to the wall. If this is not possible, step closer to the wall until you can manage. We are going to bend forward, keeping our body straight, and touching the wall with our forehead before returning back to the original position. When you can do twenty of these without a break then go on to Exercise 13b, the kneeling press up.

1	2	3	4	5	6	7	8	9	10
11	12	13	14	15	16	17	18	19	20

Exercise 13b. The kneeling press up

Kneel on the floor and put your hands in front of you. Move the hands forward as far as you can. Now dip down until the forehead and nose are touching the floor. Push back up. When you can do twenty of these without stopping, move on to the full press up.

1	2	3	4	5	6	7	8	9	10
11	12	13	14	15	16	17	18	19	20

Exercise 13c. The full press up.

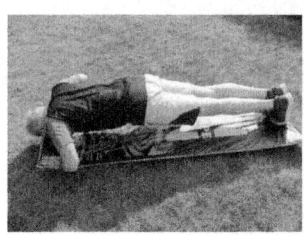  

Lie flat on the floor with your feet together and your hands below your shoulders, forehead touching the ground and on the balls of your feet. Push up until your arms are extended. Keep the back straight. Hold for a second and then slowly down touching the ground again. Hold for a second and then push back up. Repeat as many times as you can. Everyone will be different. You may only manage two or three press ups to begin with but aim to add one more every week or so. Build up to as many as you can manage but don't be surprised as you get older that you can manage less. Give yourself a reasonable target to aim for. The grid below allows for twenty but if you can manage more then do so. Breathe in as you push up and out as you go down.

1	2	3	4	5	6	7	8	9	10
11	12	13	14	15	16	17	18	19	20

Floor Exercise 14. The sit up

If doing a full sit up (exercise 14c) is not possible straight away, then build up to it by aiming to do twenty arm sit ups, (exercise 14a) then twenty hand sit ups (exercise 14b) and then finally going on to full sit ups.

Exercise 14a. Arms sit ups

 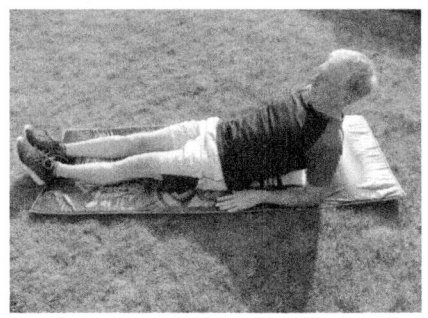

Lie flat on your back, arms by your side and then press down with your arms from the elbow down until the upper part of your body is at an angle of 45° to the floor. Hold for a second and then slowly down. Breathe in as you sit up and out as you go down. We are aiming to do 20 of these.

1	2	3	4	5	6	7	8	9	10
11	12	13	14	15	16	17	18	19	20

Exercise 14b. Hand sit ups

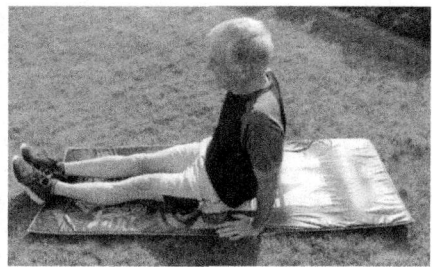

Lie flat on the floor arms by your side and then press down with your hands until the upper part of your body is at an angle of 45° to the floor. Hold for a second and then slowly down. Breathe in as you sit up and out as you go down. We are aiming to do 20 of these.

1	2	3	4	5	6	7	8	9	10
11	12	13	14	15	16	17	18	19	20

Exercise 14c. The full sit up

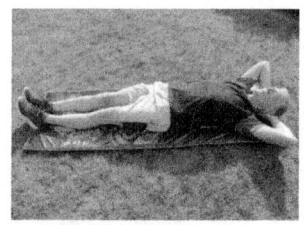

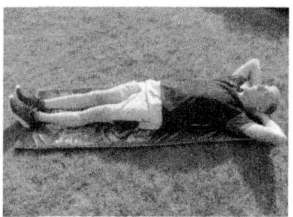

Lie flat on the floor hands behind your head and then pull yourself up to an upright position, keeping your legs flat on the floor. If it helps to keep your legs flat, hook your feet under a chair until you can keep them flat without help. Hold for a second and then slowly down. Breathe in as you sit up and out as you go down. We are aiming to do 20 of these. If you get to the stage where 20 sit ups can be done comfortably then aim to add one a week until you reach the maximum possible.

1	2	3	4	5	6	7	8	9	10
11	12	13	14	15	16	17	18	19	20

Exercise 14d. Toe touching

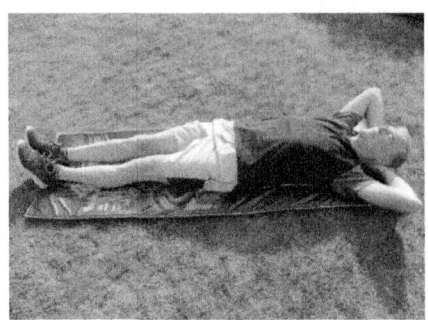

An extension to Exercise 14c for those who want to push themselves a little after achieving 20 full sit ups is to touch the toes with your fingertips when sitting up. As many as you can but aiming for twenty is a good target.

1	2	3	4	5	6	7	8	9	10
11	12	13	14	15	16	17	18	19	20

Exercise 15. The Squat

Stand with your feet shoulder width apart and your arms out in front of you and then we are going to squat down as far as we can. The aim is to get our buttocks as low to the floor as we can. Get as low as you can to begin with, without straining. Build up slowly. The aim is to be able to do 12 squats in succession. Breathe in as you squat down and out as you come up.

1	2	3	4	5	6	7	8	9	10	11	12

Now do the warm down exercises, 23 to 29

STRENGTH TRAINING WEIGHT EXERCISES

Exercising with weights is done on alternate days to Floor Exercises. See Table 3. **Never do both on the same day.**

Do the warm up exercises, Exercises 1 to 12 before you begin and the warm down exercises, Exercises 23 to 29 when you have finished.

You will eventually have to buy a set of weights consisting of two bars and 6 x 2 Kg weights and 4 x 1 Kg weights. Make sure you buy bars which have screw holders at the ends. (see illustration above). There are 'quick release' holders which have the habit after a time of releasing the weights of their own accord in the middle of your exercising and can do real damage to your legs or feet.

If you don't have your weights yet, then improvise with two plastic water bottles filled with water or two large cans from the kitchen cupboard until you have the proper weights.

If you have a set of weights, begin with just the bars. Once you can do **all** the exercises without effort, add a 1 Kg weight to each bar and do the exercises again until you can do **all** the exercises without effort again. Just to emphasise, you must be able to do all the exercises at the weight you are at so that you should not have to change the weights mid stream, once you have started the weight programme. When you can do all the exercises at the weight you are at, add on a Kilogramme weight to each bar until you reach the maximum of eight Kgs on each bar. If you get to the stage where 8 Kilograms on each bar is not enough of a challenge, then you can add more weights but don't overdo it.

The aim is to repeat each exercise until you cannot manage another one. However, if you are getting to the maximum number of repeats on all the exercises without difficulty then it is time to add a weight to the bar.

Exercise 16. Side lifts

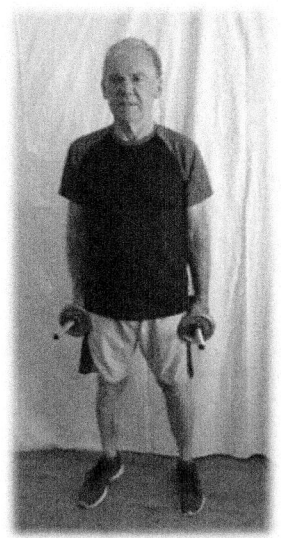  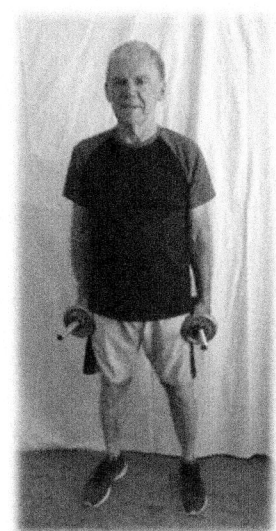

Stand with your feet shoulder width apart with the weights by your side, palms inward. Lift the weights so that they are touching your shoulders. Breathe in as you lift the weights. Hold for the count of one and then lower the weights back to your side, breathing out as you do so. Never just drop the weights. They must be under your control. Keep going to a maximum of thirty repetitions or until you can no longer lift the weights.

1	2	3	4	5	6	7	8	9	10
11	12	13	14	15	16	17	18	19	20
21	22	23	24	25	26	27	28	29	30

Exercise 17. High Lifts

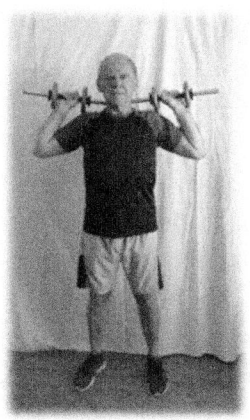

Stand with your feet shoulder width apart with the weights held at chest level, palms outward. Raise the weights above your head, arms fully stretched. Hold for the count of one and then lower the weights behind your head, hold for the count of one and return the weights above your head, hold for the count of one and then return the weights to your chest. The weights must be under control all the time Do this to a maximum of twenty times or until you can no longer lift the weights. Breathe in as you push up and out as you lower down.

1	2	3	4	5	6	7	8	9	10
11	12	13	14	15	16	17	18	19	20

Exercise 18. Front Lifts

Stand with your feet shoulder width apart with the weights held in front of you at arms' length, palms up. Lift the weights so that they are touching your shoulders. Breathe in as you lift the weights. Hold for the count of one and then lower the weights back down, breathing out as you do so. Never just drop the weights. They must be under your control. Keep going to a maximum of thirty repetitions or until you can no longer lift the weights.

1	2	3	4	5	6	7	8	9	10
11	12	13	14	15	16	17	18	19	20
21	22	23	24	25	26	27	28	29	30

Exercise 19. Dips

 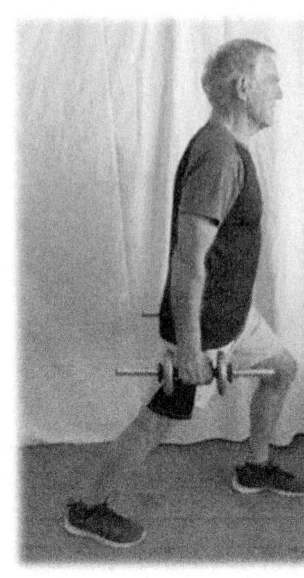 

Stand feet slightly apart with the weights by your side. Step forward as far as you can with the left foot, keeping the weights by your side but putting all the weight on your left foot. Hold for the count of three and then return to the original position. Breathe in as you step forward and out as you step back. Repeat for the right leg. We are aiming to do twelve of these altogether, six on each leg.

| 1 | 2 | 3 | 4 | 5 | 6 | 7 | 8 | 9 | 10 | 11 | 12 |

Exercise 20. Arm curls

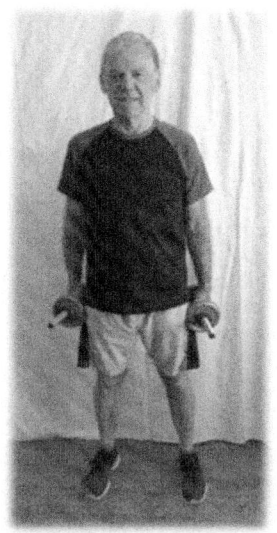 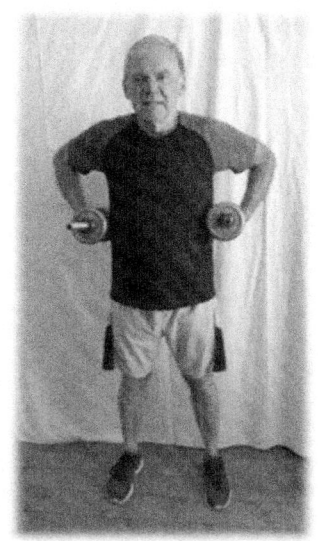 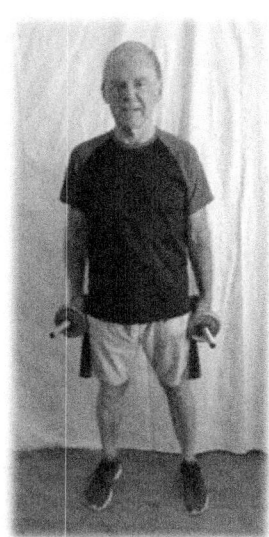

Stand feet slightly apart with the weights by your side, palms facing the body. Curl your arms inwards, raising the weights to your armpits. Hold for the count of three and then return to the original position. Don't drop the weights, keep them under control. Breathe in as you curl up and out as you curl down. We are aiming to do twelve of these.

1	2	3	4	5	6	7	8	9	10	11	12

Exercise 21. Body twists

  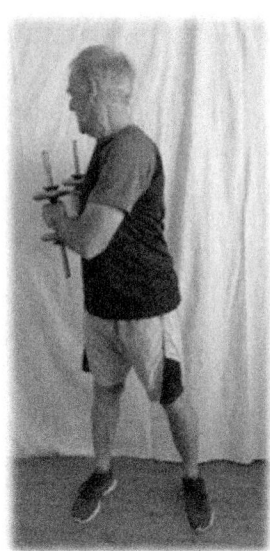

Hold the weights at chest height palms facing inward. Twist the upper body to the left and hold for the count of twelve or as long as you can. Come back to the centre and then twist the upper body to the right and hold for the count of twelve and then back to the centre. Breathe normally.

| 1 | 2 | 3 | 4 | 5 | 6 | 7 | 8 | 9 | 10 | 11 | 12 |

Exercise 22. Chest Expander

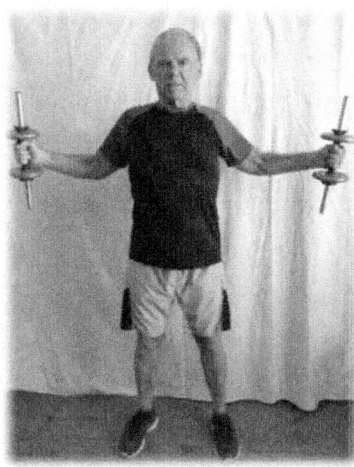

Hold the weights at chest height palms facing inward. Stretch the arms out to the side as far as you can, hold for the count of one and bring back to the centre. Breathe in as you stretch out and breathe out as you bring the weights back to the chest. We are aiming for thirty of these.

1	2	3	4	5	6	7	8	9	10
11	12	13	14	15	16	17	18	19	20
21	22	23	24	25	26	27	28	29	30

Remember, do not add any weights to the bars until you can do all the exercises, to the recommended level, in one session.

THE WARM DOWN

Now that we have done our floor or weight exercises, it is time to warm down.

Exercise 23. Leg raises

Lie on your side, legs together, one hand supporting your head, the other in front of you. Raise the upper leg as far as you can and then down again. Do this twelve times. Breathe in as you raise the leg and out as you lower it. Turn over and repeat for the other leg.

1	2	3	4	5	6	7	8	9	10	11	12

Exercise 24. Body Lifts

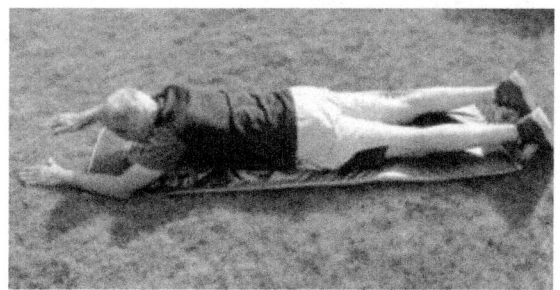

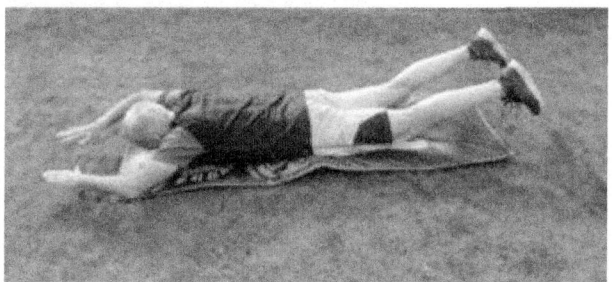

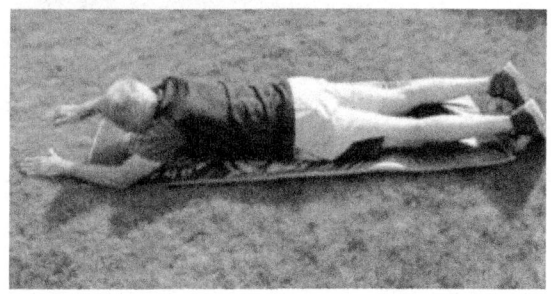

Lie flat on your stomach arms stretched out in front of you. Raise the arms as high as you can while at the same time raising both legs as high as you can. Hold for the count of two and return to the original position. Repeat twelve times or as many times as you can. Breathe in as you raise the arms and legs and out as you lower them. Aim for twelve of these.

1	2	3	4	5	6	7	8	9	10	11	12

An extension of this exercise is to raise alternate arms and legs. So raise the left arm at the same time as raising your right leg and then right arm and left leg and so on. Good for your coordination.

1	2	3	4	5	6	7	8	9	10	11	12

Exercise 25. Leg stretches

Lie flat on your stomach and get hold of your right foot with your right hand. Bring the foot as close to your right buttock as you comfortably can and hold for the count of twelve or as long as you can hold and then bring the leg back down. Breathe normally. Repeat for the left leg.

1	2	3	4	5	6	7	8	9	10	11	12

Exercise 26. Leg lifts

Lie flat on your back, cup your hands around your right knee and bring the knee as close to your chest as you can and hold for the count of twelve or as long as you can hold and then bring the leg back down. Breathe normally. Repeat for the left leg.

1	2	3	4	5	6	7	8	9	10	11	12

Exercise 27. Leg crossed lifts

Lie flat on your back, cross your left leg above your right knee and grasp your right leg under the knee. Bring your right leg as close to your chest as you can and hold for the count of twelve or as long as you can and then bring the legs back down. Breathe normally. Repeat for the right leg.

1	2	3	4	5	6	7	8	9	10	11	12

Exercise 28. Body Hug

Stand with your feet shoulder width apart and grip your left elbow with your right hand. Pull on the left arm and clench your buttocks at the same time for the count of twelve. Repeat for the other arm.

1	2	3	4	5	6	7	8	9	10	11	12

Exercise 29. Bounces

This final exercise is designed to raise your heart beat. It is quite strenuous, so begin gently and build up slowly. Stand feet slightly apart and bounce three times on the floor. On the fourth bounce lift your knees as close to your chest as you can. The aim is to touch the chest with your knees but don't be disappointed if you never reach this goal. The ultimate aim is thirty of these bounces. Try and get into a rhythm. 'One, two, three, bounce. One, two, three, bounce' etc. Breathe sharply in as you take the bounce. Take lots of deep breaths when you have finished.

1	2	3	4	5	6	7	8	9	10
11	12	13	14	15	16	17	18	19	20
21	22	23	24	25	26	27	28	29	30

A hot shower or bath after exercising is a good way to relax.

THE JOGGING PROGRAMME

The aim of this programme is to enable us to jog 5 km (3 miles) either outside or on a running machine, twice a week (see table 3). A useful motivator is to find a local 5 km fun run and set a date to join this run. Get people to sponsor you for your favourite charity and this will concentrate the mind. If you get the jogging bug, you can increase the 5 Km to any distance you are comfortable with but take it easy to begin with. 5 kilometres is a testing enough target to start with.

The first thing to do is to mark out a 5 kilometre course you are aiming to jog round. Make it as pleasant as you can, in a park or round the country lanes if you live in the country. Always jog outside in daylight hours. Jogging when it is dark is dangerous. If you are using a machine to jog then it should tell you the distances you have walked and jogged. Use a map or the milometer in your car to mark out the outdoors course.

We must be able to walk this five kilometres comfortably before we even think about jogging it. Try it and see how far you get. If you cannot yet manage to walk the full course then you need to break it down into kilometre chunks. Set the aim of walking one kilometre (half a mile). Walk half a kilometre (quarter of a mile) from the start, turn round and come back. If you get breathless, stop and get your breath back before continuing. Once you can comfortably walk one kilometre then increase to two kilometres (one mile). Walk one kilometre from the start, turn round and come back. Once you can comfortably walk two kilometres, go for three, (two miles), and then four (2 and a half miles) and finally the full five kilometres (3 miles). Use the chart below to record your progress. Don't time yourself. You are not preparing for a race.

Walk at a normal pace with the arms swinging loosely by your side. No hands in pockets or behind your back.

One Kilometre walk completed (half a mile)	
Two Kilometres walk completed (one mile)	
Three Kilometres walk completed (two miles)	
Four Kilometres walk completed (two and a half miles)	
Five Kilometres walk completed (3 miles)	

While you are building up your walking, a useful habit to get in to is to walk as much as you can in your daily life. Take the stairs instead of the lift or escalator. Do you really need to take the car to the shop down the road if you are only shopping for a few items? If you travel to work by bus can you get off a stop early and walk the last hundred metres? It all helps.

Once we can comfortably walk 5 kilometres, we are going to gradually step up to be able to jog five kilometres. Note that we are jogging not running. Jogging is a pleasant half way stage between walking and running. I am not saying, if you are capable of it, that you should not run but it is asking a lot at our age and jogging is less likely to cause any strains or injuries. Basically, we are moving along without stretching out our legs as in a run.

Not running but jogging

And one last thing, before we begin the warm ups, is about eating before jogging. Try and eat as much porridge as you can manage for breakfast. Don't jog for at least an hour after you have eaten any meal. If it fits in with your schedule, eat a medium sized banana an hour before you go jogging. This will give you an energy boost. Make the banana one of the pieces of fruit you might have eaten mid morning, so if you are going jogging later in the day, just eat one piece of fruit mid morning.

PRE JOG WARM UPS

We began our jogging programme with walking. There was no need to do any warm up exercise before a walk. We began slowly and warmed up naturally. However, when we progress to jogging, it is essential to warm up and warm down properly. The following warm up exercises should be done before setting out on our first jog and the warm down exercises done after we have completed the jog. They are essential. Do not be tempted to skip them. Setting out on a jog with cold muscles is a recipe for strain and injury.

Exercise 30. Body stretch

This is the same as Exercise 1 but it is set out again here for convenience.

(a)   (b)   (c)   (d)

(a) Stand up straight with your hands cupped in front of you, feet shoulder width apart. (b) With your body fully relaxed, bend over and see how close to the ground you can get your cupped hands. As you bend down, take a deep breath. Legs kept straight, not bending. Don't worry if you can only reach a short way down. You will get closer to the ground as we progress. (c) After a second or two, slowly raise your arms, turning your hands over and back behind your head, exhaling as you go up. Stretch your whole body. Clench your buttocks and feel the stretch in those nice straight legs. (d) Back to the start position. That's one movement. Let's see if you can do this five times. If you manage less than this, don't worry but see how many you can comfortably do. The final target to aim for is twelve stretches. Keep a record of how many stretches you do on the following table. If you manage all twelve, then concentrate on the quality of your stretches. Reach further down towards the ground and stretch further back. Take it easy. Don't strain anything.

1	2	3	4	5	6	7	8	9	10	11	12

Exercise 31. Knee raise

Standing feet shoulder width apart we raise our right leg as near to our chest as we can, gripping the leg under the knee to help it on its way.

Back and supporting leg kept straight. Hold for the count of one and release. Breathe in as you raise the leg and out as you lower it. Do twenty in all, alternating right and left legs.

1	2	3	4	5	6	7	8	9	10
11	12	13	14	15	16	17	18	19	20

Exercise 32. Reverse stretches

Standing feet shoulder width apart, reach behind with the left hand and grip the left foot at the ankle and bring it as near to your left buttock as you can. Hold for the count of one and release. Breathe in as you lift the leg and out as you lower it. Do twenty all together, alternate left and right legs.

1	2	3	4	5	6	7	8	9	10
11	12	13	14	15	16	17	18	19	20

Exercise 33. Front leg crosses

Standing feet should width apart, raise the left leg, grasp it with both hands at the ankle and pull it across your right upper leg as high as you can. Hold for the count of one and release. Breathe in as you raise the leg and out as you lower it. Do twenty all together, alternate right and left legs.

1	2	3	4	5	6	7	8	9	10
11	12	13	14	15	16	17	18	19	20

Exercise 34. Step forward and twist

Stand feet slightly apart, hands on hips. Step forward half a step with the left leg and then twist the upper body to the right as far round as possible. Back to the centre and step back and repeat with the right leg. Breathe in as you step forward and twist and out as you step back Twenty of these, ten on each leg.

1	2	3	4	5	6	7	8	9	10
11	12	13	14	15	16	17	18	19	20

Exercise 35. Leg swings

Stand feet slightly apart with your right hand on a chair back or holding on to a wall. Swing your right leg backwards and forwards five times at an angle of 45% and then straight on for another five as high as you can, aiming for the leg to be parallel to the ground. Repeat for the left leg. Twenty in all.

1	2	3	4	5	6	7	8	9	10
11	12	13	14	15	16	17	18	19	20

Exercise 36. Deep breaths

Finish by taking ten deep breaths, pulling your arms back as you breathe in.

AFTER JOG WARM DOWNS

When you have finished a jog you must warm down to prevent stiffness or cramps.

Exercise 37. Leg stretches.

Stand with your arms against a wall or chair back, right leg stretched out behind you. Put all your weight on the right leg, pressing back on to it and hold for the count of twelve. Repeat for the left leg.

Repeat Exercises 31 to 35 but only for ten repeats and then Exercise 36, ten deep breathes.

Take a hot shower or bath if convenient.

On the next two pages there is a check list for all the exercises. It can be scanned and blown up to a larger poster or cut out of this book and pinned up somewhere convenient so that you do not have to keep looking into the book. The numbers in brackets are the maximum number of repeats.

EXERCISE CHART

Warm Ups

Exc. 1. Body Stretch. (12)

Exc. 2. Neck Musc 1 (12)

Exc. 3. Neck Musc 2 (12)

Exc. 4. Neck Musc 3 (12)

Exc. 5. Arm Swings (12)

Exc. 6 Side Stretch (12)

Exc. 7 Dips (12)

Exc. 8 Leg Stretch 1 (12)

Exc.9 Leg Stretch 2 (12)

Exc. 10 Leg Stretch 3 (12)

Exc. 11 Side Stretch (12)

Exc. 12 Body Press (12)

Strength Training Floor Exercises

Exc. 13a Wall Press Up (20)

Exc. 13b Kneeling Press Up (20)

Exc. 13c Full Press Up (20)

Exc. 14a Arm Sit Up (20)

Exc. 14b Hand Sit Up (20)

Exc. 14c Full Sit Up

Exc. 14d Toe Touching

Exc. 15 The Squat

Strength Training Weight Exercises

Exc. 16 Side Lifts (30)

Exc. 17 High Lifts (20)

Exc. 18 Front Lifts (30)

Exc. 19 Dips (12)

Exc. 20 Arm Curls (12)

Exc. 21 Body Twists (12)

Exc. 22. Chest Expander (30)

The Warm Down

Exc. 23 Leg Raises (12)

Exc. 24 Body Lifts (12)

Exc. 25 Leg Stretches (12

Exc. 26 Leg Lifts (12)

Exc. 27 Leg Crossed Lifts (12)

Exc. 28 Body Hug (12)

Exc. 29 Bounces (30)

Jogging Programme Warm Up

Exc. 30 Body Stretch

Exc. 31 Knee Raise (20)

Exc. 32 Reverse Stretches (20)

Exc. 33 Front Leg Cross (20)

Exc. 34 Step Forward and Twist (20)

Exc. 35 Leg Swings (20)

Exc. 36 Deep Breaths ((10)

After Jog Warm Down

Exc. 37 Leg Stretches (12)

Exc. 38 Knee Raise (10)

Exc. 39 Reverse Stretches (10)

Exc. 40 Front Leg Cross (10)

Exc. 41 Step Forward and Twist (10)

Exc. 42 Leg Swings (10)

Exc. 43 Deep Breaths ((10)

BUILDING UP TO THE 5 Km JOG

Now that you can comfortably walk five kilometres, it is time to build up to be able to jog five kilometres. The worst thing you can do is attempt to jog the whole distance straight off. We need to build up slowly and patiently.

Wear the recommended proper clothing, especially foot wear.

Remember to do the warm up exercises before setting out to jog.

We are going to walk at our normal pace for twenty-one steps and then jog for four steps. Setting off like this we should be able to cover the full five kilometres. If you find it is too much then do as much jogging as you comfortably can and then finish the distance by walking. There is a lot of counting to do in your head but stick with it.

Once we can cover the full five kilometres with this combination of walking and jogging, we slowly decrease the walking steps and add some more jogs. The combinations are set out in the table below which you can mark off as you complete them. When you move up a level you might find that you cannot initially complete the full five kilometres. That is to be expected but as above, do as much as you comfortably can and then finish the distance by walking. Aim to go a little further next time out.

Do not progress too quickly. You should repeat each level at least three times before going on to the next level. It could well take you months to be able to complete the full five kilometre jog but once you can do this, how far you want to jog is up to you. Do the five kilometres and then add on another half kilometre or so and slowly build up to as far as you want to go

You will see that the jogs come in multiples of four. The reason for this is that we need to control our breathing. Not breathing properly is one of the main reasons for discomfort when jogging. We aim to breathe deeply for the count of two and blow out for the count of two. This breathing is in rhythm with our jogging. Two steps breathe in, two steps blow out. Once we have established this rhythm it will come automatically. If we jog a little faster we will breathe a little faster. Be aware of your breathing and build up this breathing/jogging rhythm so that eventually it will be automatic.

Level	Walk steps	Jog steps
1	21	4
2	17	8
3	13	12
4	9	16
5	5	20
7	0	Just jogging

Do not neglect to warm down and enjoy that hot shower.

CHAPTER 3

WELL-BEING

This chapter does not set out to tell you how to live your life. Rather it offers some thoughts and speculations about what it means to live a good life in the hope that this will stimulate reflections about your own life and how you live it. It is personal and therefore subjective but I offer it in good faith.

Perspectives

I am at the centre of the universe. Everything that happens is experienced through my senses. I see the world in three dimensions with the added dimension of time when I think about what happened in the past or what might happen in the future. Other people may be having similar experiences but I can only find out about them second-hand if they tell me about them or I read what they have written.

This is a workable, everyday view of reality. A way of seeing the world for all practical purposes and yet I am a small speck of life living on the smallest speck of a planet which is in a small galaxy on the outer edge of a vast universe, a universe about which we know very little. There may be other realities of which we can hardly conceive.

Does my life have any meaning or is everything random and without form? For Shakespeare's Macbeth life had no meaning:

> 'Tomorrow, and tomorrow, and tomorrow,
> Creeps in this petty pace from day to day,
> To the last syllable of recorded time;
> And all our yesterdays have lighted fools
> The way to dusty death. Out, out, brief candle!

Life's but a walking shadow, a poor player,
That struts and frets his hour upon the stage,
And then is heard no more. It is a tale
Told by an idiot, full of sound and fury,
Signifying nothing.'

Marcus Aurelius, a Roman Emperor writing in the second century A[D] asked the same question of himself but came up with the opposit[e] answer:

'Either a stew, an intricate web, and dispersal into atoms; or unity, order and providence. Now if the former, why do I even wish to spen[d] my time in a world compounded at random and in like confusion? .. But if the latter is true, I revere it, I stand firm, I take courage in tha[t] which directs all.'

Aurelius was a pagan who believed 'the Gods' were what 'directs al[l] yet he promoted reason and prudence as guides to living.

Are we then saying that to give our lives any meaning we have t[o] conform to some kind of religion, some set of prescribed beliefs tha[t] will show us the way to live our lives and preferably reward us wit[h] everlasting life when we die?

For thousands of years this was so. Most events and natur[al] occurrences such as wind and lighting could not be explained in pre[-] scientific times. Men imagined gods or a God to explain th[e] inexplicable. Priests were kept by society to explain the gods and lea[d] the worship and sacrifices that were seen as the way to keep the god[s] happy and on our side when it came to growing crops or making u[s] fertile or ensuring success in business.

Although the Greeks had their gods, they asked questions about th[e] world around them and about the way they should live their lives. [It] was this questioning spirit which was revived from the fourteent[h] century onwards and which resulted in the great scientific discoveries of our age and the questioning again by modern philosophers about man and his place in the universe. Could we meaningfully live our lives without the need for God or gods?

It was Darwin's discoveries about evolution, set out in his book 'The Origin of Species' which did much to undermine religious belief and belief in the Bible as 'the word of God'. It became clear that humankind was not a special being created by a God but one of the many creatures, some of which evolved and then become extinct over the millennia. We are part of the natural order but we are unique as a species in that our intelligence has given us the capability to improve our lives by inventions and discoveries as well as to destroy the very planet we live on by nuclear war or the destruction of the climate.

We are born and we die just as every other animal or plant comes into existence and then disappears. These two events are inescapable but it is the life we lead between these two events which is the question. How are we to spend our allotted span if not worshipping a God and preparing ourselves for an afterlife?

If we put aside the notion of reincarnation, then accepting that this one life is all we have, concentrates the mind on how best to use this precious time.

By rejecting pre-packaged religions, we become a free-minded individual able to set our own achievable goals. This is what makes us human. This does not mean that we become self-centred egoists but on the contrary, we can live in a spirit of shared humanity, developing the values of kindness and tolerance and enjoying all the things that make life beautiful and satisfying.

Unlike religions which are exclusive to the believers, humanism offers a universal way of living based not on supernatural beliefs but on a global ethic which anyone can accept, based on a generous view of human nature and needs.

Following the humanist tradition can mean a life of service to our fellow humans. We strive to give meaning to our lives by enriching our own lives and bettering the lots of those less fortunate than ourselves. There is a fine tradition of generosity of both time and money in this country. We start by improving our own lives, then our families, then the people who live in our town or city, then our country and from there the world.

How do we better our own lives? Being a humanist means being open to other ways of seeing life through music, art, literature, conversation and travel. We can even tolerate those of a religious viewpoint as long as this does not lead to violence or sexual perversion as it so often, regrettably does.

Taking just a little time each day to listen to music, read a book, look at a photograph or painting, watch a film or television programme or go to a football match will enrich our lives and widen our experiences of how other people live and think. It will make us examine our own lives and make us more tolerant of others who are different. Going out to the cinema, theatre or sports events will let us enjoy these experiences in the company of others which enriches the experience for us all.

I am not going to produce long lists of books to read or films to watch. The book shops and internet are full of suggestions and everyone has their own favourites and tastes. Just take that time to relax and enjoy what the world of the arts has to offer in this country.

Being Happy

When asked what they want from life for themselves and their children, many people answer that they want 'to be happy'. This, of course, begs the question of what we mean by 'being happy'.

Shopping might make you happy but I can think of nothing worse. Whereas, what makes me happy may be dangerous or might make someone else extremely sad or angry. There is no universal recipe for happiness. Money will not automatically make for happiness for many rich people turn out to be miserable although for some, an increase in wealth will alleviate hunger or homelessness which can increase the sense of well-being. To say that we are happy when pursuing our goals does not really help because the goals we are pursuing can be evil as well as good.

In the end happiness is directly associated with the type of life we lead. If we live a life involving respect and concern for others, a life in which we try to improve ourselves and to use such gifts as we have for the sake of others as well as ourselves, then we are likely to be on the road to leading a happy life.

Money

One of the main factors which cause people to worry and perhaps stay awake at night is money or more specifically the lack of it. There have been times in most people's lives when they have had money worries, especially if they have become unexpectedly unemployed and they have a mortgage and a family to support. I am not a money expert but *Citizens' Advice* offers a free service to anyone in money difficulties. They will offer impartial advice on the help available.

We are fortunate to live in a socialist society where it is accepted by most people that we care for our fellow citizens when they are in need. We pay through the tax system for a health service, schools and all the other services we so readily take for granted amongst them a welfare system that helps out when things go wrong. This is a precious system built up over a century and which we must safeguard from those who attack it – usually people who have no money worries.
There are however, a few basic rules to managing money which anyone can follow.

1. Live within your income.
This is easier said than done if you have a small income and many demands on your money but the principle remains the same whatever your income. If you have £600 a month income and spend £599 then you will be happy. If you spend £601 then you will be unhappy, to paraphrase Charles Dickens.
2. Prioritise your spending
There are certain things which are essential and some which are only desirable. The essential things are a roof over our heads, food on the table, warmth in the cold months and caring for our children if we have them. Once these are covered, any money left can go on the desirable items such as entertainment and extra clothing.
3. Don't fill your life with unnecessary things. We live in a society which pressurises us to buy products which we could live without. Cars, fancy watches and beauty products to name just a few. After all who cares whether Nelson Mandela wore a Rolex? It is not what he will be remembered for.

Make a will. If you have something to leave then make a will. Not doing so can create problems when you die. Making a will can help bring peace of mind.

Sleep

Getting enough quality sleep is important for our sense of well-being. Lack of sleep can be caused by physical problems and these need to be looked at by a doctor but there are some common-sense things we can do to help ensure a good night's sleep.

1. *Exercise Earlier in the day*. If you are following the exercises in this book, you have this one covered.
2. *Avoid Big Meals and Alcohol Right Before Bed*. Again, if you are following the advice on diet in this book you will be all right.
3. *Turn off your electronics*. Don't look at a screen at least an hour before going to bed.

4. Keep your bedroom at around 18°C (65° F)
5. Get a decent mattress, sheets and pillows.
6. Keep your room dark and quiet.

Smoking

If you are still smoking at this stage in your life, giving up is not going to be easy. However, there is probably no more single action that you could take that would be more beneficial to your health and well-being than giving up the habit. If nothing else, at least you should be trying to cut back. The National Health Service has a course of action which can help you quit so get in touch with your local surgery and book an appointment. You have nothing to lose and a lot to gain.

The Married Life

Social patterns have changed remarkably in our life time. Being married once meant that ideally a man and a woman fell in love, felt passionately about each other and then married in a church or registry office to give their feelings legal status and to declare their new commitment to family and friends. They set up life and home together and perhaps had children. They hoped to grow old together and remain equal friends and companions when the initial passion which drew them together had waned somewhat. They drew pleasure and contentment watching their children and grandchildren growing up as they once grew up.

Now, many couples refuse to marry at all seeing marriage as an outdated institution, more to do with contracts and legal matters than human intimacy. Homosexual and Lesbian couples marry in church and adopt children. Divorce and infidelity are rife as are marriages which for all intents and purposes have broken down.

It may be that the ideal of romantic companionship is in such trouble because it cannot encompass the storms of diverging sexual needs in a marriage. People develop and grow at different rates and the idea companion of our youth can seem infuriatingly conservative and set in their ways in middle age. Couples compromise for the sake of the marriage but sometimes the compromises can seem too high a price to pay. Young children in the marriage complicate matters immensely and most married people do all they can to protect them when parents fall out.

We have to accept that not all marriages will work out all the time and that some people are better apart than together. Those blessed with marriage which has grown and matured and remained nurturing and loving for a lifetime must count themselves among the happiest of people.

Sex

We are unfortunate in the UK in being part of the Abrahamic tradition of Judaism, Christianity and Islam which has declared taking pleasure in and rejoicing in the sexual act to be a sin. The body is of the earth and the soul of heaven and we should concentrate on the latter and control or deny the former says the Bible and Koran. Added to this the later attitude of the Puritans who thought that having sex for anything other than reproduction was a mortal sin and we have a recipe for sexual deviation and repression which has lasted for centuries. Fortunately, there are signs that these moribund attitudes are changing and that the West is rejoining the open liberal attitudes to sex of the rest of the non-Abrahamic world. Our televisions, cinema, books and theatres are now free to include the sexual side of characters where once they dare not. Young people talk openly about sex and their sexual needs in a way which shocks their grandparents not their parents.

The down side of this new liberal attitude to sex is the success of the pornography industry which has invaded the internet. Pornography should be distinguished from eroticism. Eroticism celebrates the joy of sex in the context of a fully developed character or relationship. Pornography merely concentrates on the mechanics of the sexual act, usually out of any context of mutual passion or sympathy. That is its danger when it is viewed by young people or the vulnerable. The physical act of sex itself is seen out of all context to a real relationship and can distort the young viewers ability to build such relationships of which sex is just a part, if an important part.

Of course, as we get older and the raging hormones of our younger days have settled down and thoughts other than sex and how to get it fill our minds, then we can be more relaxed about sex and perhaps even enjoy it more, rather like the occasional glass of good wine rather than a night of heavy drinking.

Older couples have to adapt and be sympathetic to their partners' current needs which may be different to their own. Some societies are quite open to the possibilities of mistresses or prostitutes who have been called 'an effective and long-standing friend to marriage'.

As the years pass, we might finally find ourselves on our own. The loss of daily companionship and intimacy can be depressing. Some find the single life a pleasure but the success of dating sites on the internet seems to show that even in our senior years, the need for companionship and sexual pleasure continues until we can do no more.

Retirement

The best advice ever given about retirement was, 'don't'. There is a difference between giving up work and retiring from life. Giving up work can be a shock to the system when the pressure, responsibility and status can disappear overnight to be replaced by endless days and night of boredom. On the other hand not having to spend one's time earning a living can open up whole new fields. Time to read, study, attend classes, start new hobbies, meet new people, get interested in politics, go to the theatre or music concerts, go on long walks – the possibilities are endless. Those who fill their retired years with purposeful activity seem to be much happier and live longer than those who don't.

Age

Growing old is not a matter of counting the years. Some people are old at twenty, others are still young at ninety. It is a matter of attitude which is under our own control. If this book has helped you to stay physically healthier and mentally active, then it has helped you to grow older more gracefully. As we get older we should get wiser and our bank balances should improve; both are desirable things.

Death and Assisted dying

Death is inevitable. It is perhaps something we don't like to think about but when our childhood heroes or people younger than us start to die, it begins to impinge on our everyday thoughts. Ideally, we would like a quick and painless death or at least a death where we dreamily drift off surrounded by our loved ones. Let us hope this is so. It is doubtful if there is any existence after death, despite what the religious community tell us. It is the quality of life which is the sacred thing, not its mere quantity.

Unfortunately, for many people the final years are filled with pain or perhaps worse than this, dementia or Alzheimer's disease take hold and life is lived without knowing who or where we are or who the people who come to visit us are.

We need to ask ourselves whether we wish to go on living as long as the medical and social services can let us or whether we would want to end our lives in a peaceful, painless and dignified way. If we take the decision that our lives are too painful or that the first signs of dementia have taken hold and it is time to draw our lives to a close, then doing so is not easy in this country.

The law at present does not allow for assisted dying and people have to travel to countries such as Switzerland to die as they wish. Anyone who helps someone to die could find themselves in trouble with the law.

Until the law is modified, each individual could make their own preparations to end their life in a way that helps them escape suffering and indignity at a time and place of their own choosing.

Printed in Great Britain
by Amazon